Signs Along The Path To Awakening

Signs Along The Path To Awakening

Anything is possible with love.
The healing of humanity lies within you.

David John Modica

Published by Tablo

Copyright © David John Modica 2020.
Published in 2020 by Tablo Publishing.

All rights reserved.

This book or any portion thereof may not be reproduced or used in any manner whatsoever without the express written permission of the author except for the use of brief quotations in a book review.

Publisher and wholesale enquiries: orders@tablo.io

20 21 22 23 LSC 10 9 8 7 6 5 4 3 2 1

To my best friend, Dawn Howard,
without whom my path would be incomplete.

And

To my dear cousin, Rocky Muzzin,
you are missed deeply by many
and you live on in our hearts.

Signposts & Pointings

The Path Of Life

This book is about the path you are on, the path of life. It seems to be a twisty road with pitfalls and waterfalls, sunshine and rain, joy and pain. It is filled with many seasons in which we are meant to learn and grow. In our experiences we are meant to transform so we become our own light and a light unto humanity.

Think of each writing in this book as "signposts" or "pointings," as I like to call them along this path. As you reach the signpost, pause and ponder what the writing is pointing to. Remember this is your path, and it is the path of your life. You are on it right now. What are you thinking? What are you feeling? Are you aware you are even thinking and feeling at all?

We experience heartache and loss, happiness and attainment, and triumph and disappointment. We experience a myriad of trials, tests, and tribulations. We may pass, and we may fail, and we have done both. All the while, whether pass or fail, we then continue to the next venture, be it a struggle or joy, and we continue this path that we call our life.

This book may come to you because you have reached the point on your path where you are questioning the purpose of it all. It may be that you have yet to ask what the meaning of it all is or if a meaning even exists. Well, I have great news for you. There is a meaning and there is a purpose to it all. YOU are the meaning, and YOU are the purpose!

A Higher Level Of Consciousness

The pointings in this book are meant to draw you into a higher world, a higher level of consciousness. This is not done with the mind, rather it is realized in and with the heart. At the very center-point of being we are the very aspect of an awareness that is alive in the consciousness of love.

The consciousness of love does not think about itself. It is a spontaneous ever-evolving creation that is an omnipresence of benevolence, compassion, empathy, kindness, and inspiration. In other words, it is everything good, and yet it is actually much more than that. For the sake of this book and what I am pointing to this is a good foundation to ignite an understanding of who and what we are. As we get closer and closer to this understanding, meaning and purpose will be revealed to you.

This is an experiential understanding that takes place within your heart. The pointings in this book are to remind you of your true self which lies within the center-point of being. It is within everyone. It is the center-point of humanity, the heartbeat of life.

What We Have Forgotten

This book was written in a way that you can pick it up and read any page in it at any time and just sit with what it is pointing to. Again, these pointings are to remind us of who and what we are. They are at a higher level of "conscious being" rather than the current understanding that brings us heartache, disappointment, and pain. This current understanding resides in thought and thought only, and thought is unaware of itself. How can something that is unaware of itself ever rest in the peace of knowing itself? It can't.

As an example, you pick up the book as you are struggling with a crisis of some kind, and you read "The more you can learn to be an observer of thought rather than identifying with it the less it has its hold on you." This one sentence is enough to reexamine and even end the crisis which began in our mind. We suffer because we are unconsciously identified with ourselves absorbed in thought. We think it is actually us thinking and it is not. This is what we have forgotten.

Maybe you read "The peace you seek lies in the consciousness of your heart. Let love's consciousness awaken you to abandon all thoughts you have about yourself and of life. Surrender. This is the path of negation. This is the path of love's conscious transformation." This pointing speaks to the heart of who and what you are. You are the consciousness of love, not a product of thought in a moment of time. Allow this pointing to penetrate your being, and let it act upon you. It is meant to take you out of the time world of thought to the door of who and what you are. Here, meaning and purpose are revealed to you. This meaning and purpose is not of the mind but of the heart, the consciousness of love.

The Consciousness Of Love

You have a soul. It is the connecting point between the heavens and the earth, that which is immortal and mortal. You are a spiritual being temporarily in the form of a body on this planet called earth. We are called to love by the consciousness of love itself for the sake of our soul's development. We are meant to live as fully awake, conscious human beings in union with the divine. We have been designed to create for the good of humanity, not to destroy.

Ultimately, we are to discover we are pure love created by pure love. Humanity has strayed from this understanding, which is the original meaning of the word "sin," or the Hebrew word "hata," which literally means "going astray" or "to miss the mark." This book is meant to point you in the direction of your purpose and meaning in this life. It is not to tell you what your meaning and purpose are, rather for you to discover and allow it to be revealed to you.

Your Awakening

Your path is of the consciousness of love, whether you realize it or not. Your existence on this planet at this time is temporary, but the consciousness of love will always be, for it is eternal. The consciousness of love will always beckon you. It speaks directly to your heart, for it exists within your heart. We are meant to understand our lives from and within this higher consciousness rather than the non-understanding of the one we suffer in and from currently.

As you ponder the pointings in this book and do your best to be aware of the signposts along your path with earnest effort, you allow your heart to receive and your mind to follow. You will experience a transformation.

It is the experiential transformation and the transcendence of a heart now guiding the mind in union with the divine, the consciousness of love. Here, it is revealed to you that your path is a creation in alignment with God. Meaning, purpose, contentment, and joy all reside within your heart with the awareness that belongs to the consciousness of love.

1 ~ Waking Up From a Dream

Waking up in this life
is no different than waking up from a dream.
Everything in the dream is over
and going back to serve the dream has no meaning
and serves no purpose.

Embrace your awakening!

2 ~ This Is Our Calling

Suffering will cease when you fully serve your heart.
Your heart is the center-point of being.
The mysterious truths of the cosmos all lay within your heart
for that is where you come from.
The cosmos, your heart, they are identical.

Serve your heart and you serve the cosmos.
This is our calling.
Each individual actuated by the divine cosmic multiverse,
the consciousness of love.

The cosmos is divinity in action and has given rise to you.
Know this and rest in its serenity of being.
This is the healing and transformation of humanity.
To serve your heart is to serve all mankind,
even though it may be understood by few.

We have forgotten that we are meant to be
a benevolent and empathetic humanity.
We have forgotten we are of one consciousness,
and we belong to each other.

Return to what has been forgotten.
Serve and live in the consciousness of love.

3 ~ This Life

When you realize that this life
is not actually about this earthly existence
then the purpose of your life changes dramatically.

4 ~ A Higher Vibration

Happiness and contentment do not come
from what you have or do not have.
Happiness and contentment belong to a human being
who lives from the consciousness of the heart.

You have the eyes to see and the ears to hear
a higher vibration of reality than that of an unconscious,
rambling mind filled with thoughts.
This awareness is the foundation of the consciousness of love.

This is the ground from which we were meant
to breathe, speak and act.
The human being who lives so acts for the good of humanity.

Happiness and contentment flow hand in hand
with benevolence and compassion.
Love flows easily because one is actuated
by the consciousness of love itself.

Live here and every day will be a birth into a new life.

5 ~ Heart and Soul

Your inner awareness of your own suffering
is the door to awakening.
At the center-point of being,
this silent awareness is the nourishment
of your heart and soul.

6 ~ Field of Creation

You are a being of creation in a field of creation
connected through conscious thought and action.
This is the ever-expanding field of the consciousness of love
of which all things are connected.

We exist in this field of energy in communion with each other.
We are unlimited and without boundaries.
An awakened being exists consciously
at the center-point of being,
and is in communion with the whole field.

Thought and action guided by the heart are
benevolent, kind, compassionate, and encouraging.
The whole field is affected by an awakened being
and this individual creates for the good of all humanity
and the cosmic whole.

There is not a single action that is not of love.

7 ~ Thoughts

The only struggle any human being has
is with their own thoughts.
There is no struggle outside of this.

8 ~ I AM

Self-discovery is actually the discovery
of being that which is selfless.

I AM is all there is.
I AM is the cosmic whole.
I AM is the center-point of being.
It's everywhere and everything
and it's ever-expanding.

To live from the center-point of being
is to live beyond thought,
and in the direct alignment with the eternal I AM,
the consciousness of love.

The key to the door of this direct alignment lies within you.

9 ~ To Be Awakened

One cannot know what it means to be awakened
without fully understanding
their own suffering.

10 ~ The Field of Existence

When truly living in the moment
an awakened human being is dictated
by the consciousness of love.
There is nothing to hold onto, nothing to control,
and nothing to want or avoid.

The awakened individual receives endless gifts
of higher wisdom.
In direct alignment with the heart,
the center-point of being is without any suffering or confusion.

Our true human potential lies in our willingness to abandon
our intellectual knowledge and remain in the unknown,
undefinable presence of silence and stillness.
Here, one sees that everything is connected,
from the most minute particle to the farthest star.

We are in relationship with a complete field of existence
that is wholly alive and is of one entity.
This field is an endless creation,
and we are intimately tied to it with our thoughts and actions.

Every thought and every action is a spark of creation
that ripples through the space-time continuum.
We emanate energy and it speaks to the cosmic whole.
Here, the awakened individual lives in the peace
of the energetic field of awakened consciousness,
the consciousness of love.

11 ~ The Healing of Humanity

The healing of humanity's illnesses all reside
within the awakened heart giving rise to an illumined mind.

12 ~ Love Is Beyond Thought

The inner eyes that see things as they are
without any judgment
awaken an individual to the understanding
of the suffering of humanity.

A human being suffers to the exact degree
that they are identified with their thoughts.

To observe thought is to stand on the ground of consciousness.
To remain on this ground is to awaken.
The awakened individual is in alignment
with the consciousness of love.

Love is beyond thought and without self-reference.
The heart of the human being that lives here
thrives in this life and loves ardently and eternally.

13 ~ You Are the Eyes

You are the eyes through which
the consciousness of love sees itself.

14 ~ One Main Purpose

Your heart is infinitely more powerful than your mind.

At the center-point of being fully awake,
in and from the consciousness of love,
we see we are everything and infinite,
where there is no birth, no death, and far beyond thought.

From this place, our true nature does not think about itself,
rather we are an action of an endless awakening
in an eternal movement with one main purpose, love.

A mind in alignment with the heart and consciousness of love
is a beacon unto itself and humanity.
The light within the heart, by its very nature,
must penetrate the dark both inwardly and outwardly.

This is our calling.

The healing of humanity rests within each individual.
We are called to be the action and creation
of the consciousness of love.

We are called to love.

15 ~ An Illumined Mind

An awakened heart gives rise to an illumined mind.

16 ~ Meaning and Purpose

To abandon yourself is to find yourself.
Abandon all that you have thought about yourself
and reach the root of what is there.

In the silent depths of being
lies the ever-present consciousness of love,
the fierce awareness of self.
Here, the chaotic mind is a distant past.
The eyes that see with instant understanding belong to love.
You are this love.

The clarity of the consciousness of love
dwells within all human beings.

We must return to our natural consciousness.
This consciousness not only rules over the chaotic mind
but guides the mind into direct alignment with the heart,
the center of being.

This alignment is the healing and flourishing of our divine life.
For one that lives in and from the consciousness of love
there is not a moment without meaning and purpose.

17 ~ An Awakened Human Being

With an endless presence of peace
and with the speech of kindness and encouragement
an awakened human being harms no one.

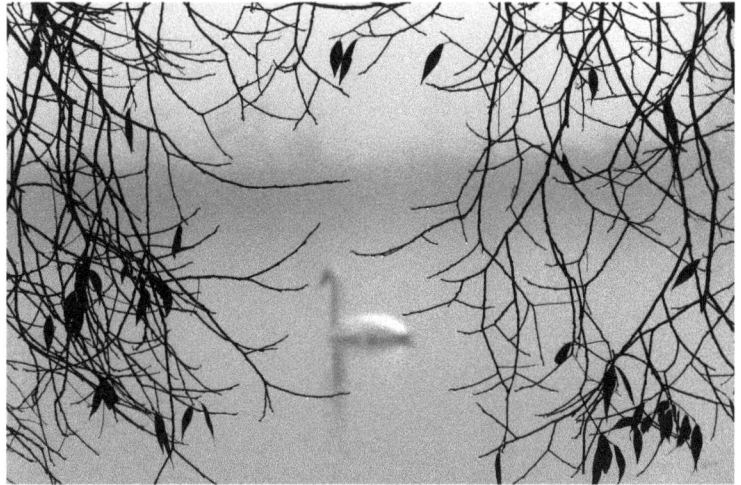

18 ~ I AM LIFE

Think of yourself as consciousness
and develop this habit for it's the truth.

Do this more and more
and you will think of yourself less and less as a person
or even the human body.

We are consciousness, spirit, and this is eternal.
The physical form is temporary.

Eventually, you'll see everything as consciousness,
and it's there we are aligned with God.

Here, we see I AM LIFE,
and therefore it cannot be against us.
Hence, you will create your path and your life accordingly.

This is the power you have.
This is the power of the consciousness of love.

19 ~ The Peace You Seek

The peace you seek lies in the consciousness of your heart.
Let love's consciousness awaken you
to abandon all thoughts you have about yourself and of life.
Surrender.
This is the path of negation.
This is the path of love's conscious transformation.

20 ~ You Are the Action

Thoughts of sadness search for happiness,
but happiness has nothing to do with thought.
You cannot think yourself into happiness
nor can you find happiness outside of you.

Happiness resides in the awareness of the consciousness of love.

From here you have the power to observe yourself
and all humanity and beyond.
Here is where it is realized for you.
You are the action of happiness, peace, and joy.

Such is the consciousness of love.

21 ~ Lighting Your Path

You are not lost in the dark.
You are the light shining in the dark,
and you are lighting your path before you.

22 ~ Epicenter of Consciousness

In reality, you are the epicenter of consciousness.
Consciousness is presence and presence is now.
Be here now not with thought but with your heart.
Presence IS your heart.

You are an emerging possibility of endless creation
wherein your heart within the consciousness of love
is your guidance.

All that is good resides in the center-point of being,
here and now.

Ultimately, it is your destiny
to awaken and return to what you already are,
the epicenter of the consciousness of love.

23 ~ Realized in Love's Consciousness

The heart of a human being
fully realized in love's consciousness
puts that individual on a path of pure joy and contentment.
Love lights a path beyond thought.

24 ~ Love's Awareness Within You

A negative thought stands alone
until you identify with it.
Leave it be.
You have the power to watch it pass.
This is an action
of the consciousness of love's awareness within you.

Love has enabled you with the ability to let go
as you discern with the eyes of love within you.

Love has no limits.
Limits exist in the mind and the mind only.
What you think you can and cannot do
exist only in unconscious thought.

When this is seen clearly,
then one sees through success and failure as there is neither.
There is only the action of doing in the moment
within the awareness of the consciousness of love.

Love is without comparison and judgment,
and love never hinders.

25 ~ Without Thought

You won't know who you are
until you meet yourself without thought.

26 ~ Benevolence and Guardianship

The consciousness of love lives in the hearts of all human beings.
We actually think from our heart-center without words
only to have thought follow.

When you live from the consciousness of love
thought is observed, discerned, and dismissed.
Here, the mind is actuated to serve the heart.

At the center-point of being one lives from the awareness
of the consciousness of love.
To not live from this center-point
one serves a mind lost in imagination.
We believe in its limits and its judgments,
and we believe this thinking is actually "me."
It is not.

Who you truly are is a creation of the divine
with the ability to observe and discern your thoughts
and to consciously choose your role in this life
for the benevolence and guardianship of humanity.

27 ~ Within You

The light you are looking for that lights the world is within you.

28 ~ Expand the Cosmic Whole

Our actions matter, for we are of one consciousness.

Through my speech and actions,
rooted in love and compassion,
humanity is touched.

This contribution allows for goodwill and harmony
to expand the consciousness of humanity
and the cosmic whole.

There is not a single aspect of creation that is left untouched.

29 ~ What You Create

Be conscious of what you speak for that is what you create.

30 ~ A Candle that Lights the Dark

Love is at the center of your being.
Love has the answer and love is what you are.

This means you have the answer
and you have the power to know who and what you are.

You have the power to consciously create your life.
and fill it with the essence of love.

Touch humanity every moment with your being
like a candle that lights the dark.

31 ~ Intimately Connected

One's awareness of self
is also the awareness of the cosmic whole.
They are one and the same and intimately connected.

32 ~ The Journey Back Home

Love's consciousness and actions exist
within every human being.
The journey back home to love is inward.

You'll know you are getting close the more you realize
you are the observer and the observed.

Love doesn't call itself anything
for love is a pure act of conscious being, egoless.

This is freedom from all the ties that bind us
to worldly thinking.
Here, one lives in consciousness in alignment with God's will.

33 ~ Look Inward, Remain Silent

The key is to look inward, remain silent, and stay there.

34 ~ Catalyst for Change

Inner conflict is the catalyst for change within yourself.
Inner conflict is a sign you are out of balance.
To resist the conflict actually keeps the conflict in place.
The resistance and conflict are one action.

Standing within the foundation of love
and with the eyes to see and the ears to hear,
you will see you are not your thoughts
that keep the conflict in place.

Love allows us to let the thoughts be there,
and love's eyes of awareness keeps you unidentified
with the swirling thoughts.

Like the eye within the hurricane,
you are centered within the consciousness of love itself.

35 ~ Your Mind's True Role

Your mind's true role is to serve your heart.

36 ~ Live From Your Heart

Don't be concerned with your thoughts.
Live from your heart.
Your mind was created to follow your heart.
Leave your thoughts alone.

The highest order of thinking
rests within the awareness of the consciousness of love.
Here we receive that which cannot be put into words.
Here we are the living action of benevolence,
compassion, empathy, and kindness.

There is nothing more important
that you can do for yourself and humanity
than to walk the path of your life
within the consciousness of love.

This is the path of peace and healing
and this path touches the whole of humanity.

37 ~ Let Go

Go ahead, let go... love will catch you.

38 ~ As A Child

Turn your eyes and ears inward.
Watch and listen.

You will discover you have unconsciously handed your life over
to a mind filled with concepts and images
that you have thought so many times have long since become
mechanical actions that move you through life,
tainting almost everything you see,
every action you take,
and every word you speak.

Thought cannot provide the answer to suffering
as it is the identification with thought
that is the cause of suffering.
Beyond thought is love.
Love's actions are egoless and spontaneous.

Return as a child back to the source and consciousness of love.
Love would like to welcome you back home.

39 ~ Stop Running

When we stop running
from what we are afraid of seeing in ourselves
we will discover the unlimited power and beauty
of who and what we are.

40 ~ Find Yourself

To abandon yourself is to find yourself.
More and more, as you are able to see thought
without being thought,
you are, by this action of seeing,
in the space of observing and discerning.
This is sacred ground within you.
This is also the natural inner home of your beingness.
You are a loving, whole and holy being.

The chaotic mind suffers in trying to be at peace with itself.
When observed from the natural home of beingness within you,
the ability to discern thought now enables thought
to be guided by the consciousness of love.
You are now abandoning what has never been you,
and this abandonment leads you home to who you truly are,
which is undefinable by thought.

You are a free and conscious human being.
You have the ability to actuate your life as you please.
In this, your life now has become the good for all things.
You serve humanity because you serve the consciousness of love.
This is what it means to abandon yourself,
and you will find yourself.

41 ~ Infinite Wisdom

Your true nature
is the consciousness of infinite wisdom and love
untouched by the mind.

42 ~ This Is Our Gift

Love was placed inside you before you were born,
and that is to seek itself in this human form.
To reach for the understanding of love and to live from love
is the foremost reason why we are here.

To truly know yourself and live from the consciousness of love
is to be without a trace of malice or ill will.
To know yourself is to love yourself.
Love yourself in this way, and humanity will start to heal.

This is our gift,
this is our action,
and this is our completion.

Love.

43 ~ Seek to Understand

Seek to understand love at its fullest,
all other endeavors pale in comparison.

44 ~ Love is Existence

Happiness resides in the consciousness of love.
This is your true nature.
The center-point of awareness
with its ability to observe without attachment
is the ground of pure being.

Be here as an action of the consciousness of love.
This action permeates the cosmos.
The cosmos is aware of you, and you are aware of it.
With this understanding, kindness, and compassion
is without exception.

Love is existence.
The ever-expanding cosmic whole
is the ever-expanding existence of the consciousness of love.
Here and beyond, all exist in the heartbeat of love,
the divine creation of the divine creator.

45 ~ To Live Consciously

To live consciously has no demand on others.
This is the peace of living within the consciousness of love.

46 ~ The Root of Awakening

The true crisis humanity is experiencing
is the inability to understand its true nature,
the consciousness of love.

One must allow themselves to be called upon
and into this alignment.
It is our highest responsibility
and reveals a life of unlimited possibilities.

Lay your life down for the sake of love's consciousness.
The consciousness and awareness of love are beyond thought.
Hence, there is no self-reference in it.
This is the root of awakening.

Get to where you have nothing left but to ask love for help,
not because you want it, rather because you need it.

Love burns brightest in one's honest surrender.

47 ~ Humanity Thirsts

See yourself as love, for that is what you are,
and give yourself away.
Humanity thirsts.

48 ~ Surrender

Eventually, the seeker will find themselves with one option left
and that is to surrender to love.
There is no other action.

In this acquiescence,
one becomes what they have always been,
the living action of love itself.

You are a celestial vibration in human form,
and you are more than capable of love's fervent path
that has been set before you.

The consciousness of love has chosen you for the task at hand.
Your destiny is before you.

49 ~ All That's Left is Love

When you come to the complete end of yourself,
to the edge of the world of thought,
you will find all that's left is love.
The consciousness of love is who and what we are.

50 ~ Love's Grace

Living from love is living from love's authenticity.
Kindness, compassion, encouragement, and forgiveness flow
from the human being self-realized in love.

Love is who and what we are,
and we are meant to walk in love's grace and tranquility.

The awakened human being is the one
who lives from love and is self-realized in love.
They are the essence of authenticity and grace.

Surrender to love for it's your destiny,
and its essence is eternal.

51 ~ A Life Not Lived

A life not lived in the consciousness of love is a life lived in vain.

52 ~ The Never-Ending Kingdom

You are not the voice in your head.
You are the spirit that gives rise to your heart.
Here, from the awareness of the consciousness of love,
one returns to thinking and acting
from the center-point of being.

This is the ground of a continual awakening,
the ground of the sacred and eternal.
Here, all thought is observed and discerned
and one acts accordingly and willingly
for the good of humanity.

It matters not what you have but what you can give.
Here, the awakened individual serves
in the never-ending kingdom
of the consciousness of love.

53 ~ The Mysterious Eternal

You are moved by the mysterious eternal.
You are moved to the core of your being because at your core you ARE the mysterious eternal.

54 ~ You Are Love's Energy and Animation

We must learn to love ourselves, not in some grandiose way.
Humbly accept yourself as an imperfect work in progress
without judgment and without denial,
to be fully aware of ourselves as we are
in this and every moment.

This action is the steadfast center-point of being.
This is where we endlessly see love in action,
a complete forgiveness of ourselves and others,
and the eternal birth of joy and contentment.

You arose from love.
Love breathes you into existence,
and you'll return to love.

You are love's energy and animation.
Love's laws are written on your heart.
The understanding of love is the understanding of yourself
for love's consciousness already dwells within you, eternally.

55 ~ Heartbeat of Life

The human being who walks the path
of the consciousness of love realizes that this path
is the heartbeat of life.
All else is secondary.

56 ~ The Path Home

It's not enough to just talk about love.
Lay down your life in agreement with love's consciousness.
Become a token of acquiescence,
and love will work its wonders through you.

Allow your mind to become perfectly still,
even if simply for a moment.
This respite allows love's consciousness
to slowly but surely remind you who and what you are
and who and what you have always been.

Remain quiet and unattached to not a single thought.
Observe your mind and serve your heart.
This is the path home to the center-point of being,
the consciousness of love.

57 ~ True Nature

Just as the nature of the sun is to shine,
the true nature of a human being is to love.

58 ~ Love Speaks Without Words

The revealing of your true self
is the revealing of your egoless essence
which belongs to the consciousness of love.

All that is good and true is without self-reference.
Allow this to penetrate your heart,
and your mind will align itself and surrender
to the consciousness of love.
Herein lies an inner and eternal foundation of peace.

The burden of thought has created the suffering of humanity.
Put the weight of this burden down.
You were never meant to carry it.

Your true self lies in the consciousness of love.
Love is beyond thought,
and love speaks without words.

To live from the awareness of the consciousness of love
is to live from your true center of being
within which lies the consciousness of God.

59 ~ A Creation of the Divine

You are not a product of thought.
You are a creation of the divine consciousness of love.

60 ~ Reborn Into Consciousness

Remain inwardly silent,
and it will be revealed to you who and what you are.

A chaotic mind cannot hide.
Observe.
A discovery awaits you.
You are not your mind.

Stay in the center of observation.
Your mind is meant to be guided by this observation.
It must yield.
This is the journey back to your true nature,
the consciousness of love.

To wake up is to fully serve the consciousness of love.
Your heart has no conflict and no enemies.
Awareness lives in the peace and freedom
of the awakened heart that guides the mind.

This is the awareness of the cosmic whole,
and you are one with the cosmic whole.
Come into this understanding and allow yourself to be
reborn into consciousness.

This is the consciousness of love, God.

61 ~ Be An Observer of Thought

The more you can learn to be an observer of thought
rather than identifying with it the less it has its hold on you.

62 ~ Serenity of Being

The light of the consciousness of love resides within you,
it is the fulfillment you yearn for.
It is far beyond thought and beyond the mind's comprehension.
Return to your heart as your heart is the home
of the consciousness of the light of love.

See that you are not your thoughts,
and you will find your thoughts are the only obstructions
to the peace and happiness of life.

Your true nature is love.
Benevolence, kindness, and compassion flow
from the deep rivers of God's consciousness
that gave rise to who and what you are.

You are a vehicle for the expression of His love
now and always,
eternally.

This is the true serenity of being.

63 ~ Joy of Being

In the absence of self-reference lies the joy of being.

64 ~ Weep With Gratitude

When understood, you should weep with gratitude
that you have been given life so divine
and a path so unique for your soul's growth.

In any moment all you see, feel, and hear
is the voice of the divine
as you are always looking at life
from the consciousness of love.

Walk in this understanding daily,
and you will touch the lives of many.
Not because you are special,
rather the consciousness of divine love
is never-endingly acting and living through you.

We are all vessels of love.
How could I possibly hurt another human being
when I live within the grace of such divine intelligence.

65 ~ Love Wants to Awaken You

Love wants to awaken you to your highest human potential
and to draw out of you all that you truly are
to transcend your falsely perceived limits.
That which rises from love is inherently unlimited.

66 ~ Awakened Eyes

With awakened eyes one sees each moment
is a doorway to the next.
Life is, from the awareness of love's consciousness,
all one moving breath of existence eternally evolving.

Every human being has a part in this transformation
whether they know it or not.
We are meant to know this and live
from the awareness of the consciousness of love.

This is where our healing as a human race starts.

Live from the serene and tranquil clarity of your heart.
Here, you will be like a child filled with innocence
that knows the safety and protection of being in the presence
of your Father's love.

67 ~ Love Has Never Left Us

If we would make love our highest priority,
we would find love has made us its highest priority.
Love has never left us.
It is we who have left love.

68 ~ Eternal Moment

The depth of the moment in all its entirety is never really seen.
One must be absolutely still and silent inwardly.
The depth of this very moment is eternal.
It has no birth and no death,
no beginning and no end,
no future and no past.
It has always been.

This moment is expanding outwardly
as it is one with the entire cosmos,
ever-changing and unfolding.
As you and I act and speak we are the creators of the cosmos
through the ripple effect of every action,
like a pebble thrown into a pond.

Every human being either adds to or subtracts from
the human consciousness.
The human being that lives from the center-point
of the consciousness of love lives in the eternal moment
of never-ending life.

All of life is connected in this eternal moment
of cosmic existence.
This is where we consciously create for ourselves
and for the good of humanity and beyond.

69 ~ Stillness and Silence

No activity can bring you to the peace of stillness and silence for stillness and silence is the ground of all activity.

70 ~ A True Miracle

When you see with your heart
that everything is connected and everything is love
you will also see you cannot harm anything
without harming yourself and humanity.
This is the experience of the consciousness of love.
Here, one lives serving mankind
with benevolence, compassion, and empathy toward all.

The consciousness of love is the highest vibration there is.
This vibration gives rise to the cosmos
and gives rise to humanity.
It is our destiny to return to this consciousness.
This understanding must be realized from within.

A true miracle is a human being so touched
by the consciousness of love that they have abandoned
all they have taken themselves to be
to simply walk in the light of love.
Here, we return to wholeness.
Here, we abandon ourselves to the consciousness of love,
and in doing so we find ourselves.
Each and every one of us is a gift of love's consciousness.

71 ~ Let Love Breathe You

Be still and let love breathe you.

72 ~ Nothing is Separate

Everything is connected and given life from the source, love.
Nothing is separate.
All is the whole.

Already, in motion are possibilities we have yet to tap into.
We are an unlimited being bound to nothing
when our mind is aligned with our heart
and the consciousness of love.

Love is the energy that ties the quantum field
of the cosmic whole together
throughout the space-time continuum.

The awakened individuals that live
in the understanding of these laws harm no one
and live and love eternally.

73 ~ One Entity

You are being breathed into existence,
and you are breathing in the consciousness of love.
Your breath and the air you breath is one entity, love.

74 ~ Direct Reception

We have forgotten that we are meant to think with our hearts, not our minds.
The direct reception of higher consciousness is in the heart.

Here, at the center-point of being,
full awareness of life is automatic and axiomatic.
Your true nature is awareness and love.
Space itself is alive with infinite currents of love
and it is love that gives rise to everything.

Life energy permeates the cosmos.
All life is a drop of consciousness within the cosmic whole.
What you speak and act ripples through the stratum of creation.
You are a vibration emanating all you think, feel, and act.

Live within the awareness of the consciousness of love,
and your vibration will strengthen and heal not only humanity
but will resonate throughout the entire cosmic whole.

75 ~ Reflect the Light of Love

Just as the moon reflects the light of the sun,
we are called to reflect the light of love.

76 ~ Faith

Faith is to surrender to the unknown.
Because there is no ego in the consciousness of love,
it is an unascertained harborage.
It's not something you can imagine and shape into a belief
structured by an accumulation of thoughts.
Faith is without self-reference and is directly connected to
the intuition of the heart.
Here, the unknown becomes known.
Within this knowing lies true faith.

Faith is revealed to the one that inhabits the natural state
of awareness at the center-point of being.
It is not "I" that have faith,
rather the I AM from which all life arises.
The consciousness of love in and of itself is faith,
the two are one.

Here, the awakened individual resides in a knowingness
directly connected to the divine.
This is an impersonal knowing
that permeates one's every thought and action.
Benevolence, kindness, compassion are never-ending.

This is the behavior of all that is good and true.
This is the faith in which love conquers all.

77 ~ Beliefs

Faith naturally arises as one sees through and let's go of all their beliefs.

78 ~ The Highest Action

There is no higher action than love.
There is no less action required as a human being.
It is the essential fulfillment of every individual on this planet
for the human race to become a conscious, compassionate,
and intelligent human being.

I am called to love.
I am alive to love.
My very being must be love,
and my life begins and ends here.

Love has faith in you.
It always has and always will.
You are not separate from love.
You are love; therefore, for love to have faith in you
means love has faith in itself.

Come to this understanding and realize
that love truly does conquer all.

79 ~ Anything is Possible With Love

Fully surrender to the call of love within you
and you will realize anything is possible with love .

80 ~ The Power to Love

Living from love is not difficult.
It has one requirement:
You must give yourself to it with nothing held back.
That is the requirement.
So every action is an action of love.
Every act is an act of creation in kindness,
compassion, and encouragement.

Living from here you find love has always been, eternal.
Living from here you will not only know love;
you become love.
You are love.

We were created as conscious and creative human beings.
We have the power to choose and to create.
We have the power to be kind and to encourage others.
We have the power to give of ourselves and help those in need.
We also have the power to let go of what hurts.

Most of all,
what we really have,
we have the power to love and be loved.

81 ~ The Love We Search For

We search for love, never realizing the love we search for we already are.

82 ~ Lift Humanity

The more you see life from the awareness
of the consciousness of love within you
the more is given you to consciously discern the thoughts
that fly through the sky of your mind,
and from there create a world of peace and unity
for yourself and humanity.

Don't let a chaotic mind distract you from the beauty of silence.
A chaotic mind is observed from the silence of beingness,
the consciousness of love.

Allow your ardent heart to shine like the sun
on all in your presence.
Lift humanity even though they may never know
it was love's consciousness living through you.

Love is without ego.
Love simply loves.

83 ~ Love is Our healing

Kindness is the greatest beauty,
forgiveness the greatest love
and love is our healing.

84 ~ Return

When you have suffered enough
with the toil of your own thoughts about life
you will see the invitation at the door of your heart
to step into love's conscious awareness.
Seize this moment.

Here, you will realize that you have the eyes to see
beyond the thoughts that currently limit you.
Return to love's conscious awareness and return home,
joyful and content in your own skin.

Freedom and happiness are not found outside of you.
Awareness is the freedom that stems
from the happiness and joy within you,
which is the consciousness of love.
You were born with this consciousness.

You have forgotten that it not only resides in you but it IS you,
like a bird wondering where the air is that it's flying in.
The air and the bird are one.

Know this and return,
and you will wake up every day with a heart so content
you will weep with gratitude.
The grace of love has brought you home.

85 ~ Answers

Every single answer lies within you.
Let go of you and answers will be revealed.

86 ~ The First Step in Forgiveness

To realize that someone hurt you
because they themselves are hurting
is the first step in forgiveness.
We hurt others because we ourselves hurt.

Forgiveness is an action that heals the whole of humanity.
That is the nature of the consciousness of love.

We must remember to be kind to ourselves,
for our heart in return will rain down its precious consciousness.
Our being will be filled with the awareness of light
that gives rise to eyes that see and ears that hear.

This is the inner journey that brings the individual home
to one's heart where the consciousness of love lives,
the center-point of the light of being.

87 ~ Forgiveness is the Love Song

Forgiveness is the love song written by God
and placed within your heart.

88 ~ Love Has Brought You Home

Consciousness exists before thought.
At the center-point of consciousness
you are given eyes to see and ears to hear,
and what you see and hear is felt in your heart.

God speaks thunderously silent to you.
Through the grace of the consciousness of love
you have been pulled out of the mire
of ordinary human thought and have been set free.

Your will has become the will of love.
Now you serve your heart and your mind follows.
You are aligned with eternal consciousness.
You are aware, awake, and everything is observed.

The consciousness of love now actuates your existence.
It breathes you, incites you, and it moves you.
Rejoice!
Love has brought you home.

89 ~ Find Me With Your Heart

You can find me with your heart.
And to find me is to discover what you are,
to know yourself as love and act accordingly,
as I will be with you everywhere and in everything.

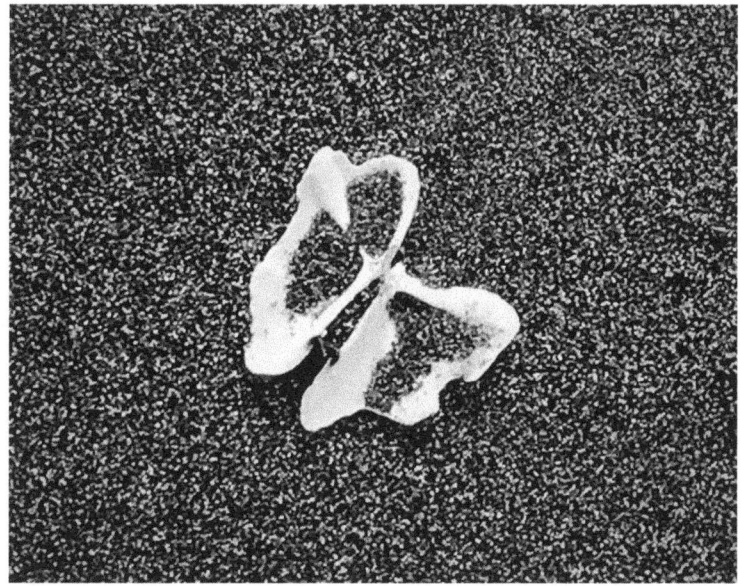

90 ~ Allow Love to Take Your Life

Live fully in the present moment.
Observe and let everything come and pass.
There's nothing to hold on to and nothing to avoid.
This is truly loving yourself and others.

To resist something negative you see within yourself
actually perpetuates its existence.
See what you see without self-reference
because it has no reality without your agreement to it.
This is the path beyond thought.
This is the path of the consciousness of love.

Allow love to take your life into its realm of vision and clarity.
Chains of limitations will disintegrate
and sorrows will turn into pearls of wisdom.

Love is who you are: a vibration in physical form
now transcending this earthly plane.
You are in this world but you are not of this world.
This is the one true freedom.

91 ~ The Search for Love

The search for love led me back to the beginning of my search.
It existed within me all along.

92 ~ Love is Eternal

Thought is time; love is eternal.

The consciousness of love is eternal
while thought enters after the physical body is born.
Thought passes with this body
while the consciousness of love, God, is eternally alive.

Our heart which is our direct center of being
is where we are to realize, understand, and receive
reality in this very moment.
This is an understanding without words.
As we come to this understanding
the mind will follow as it is intended.
This is the mind's rightful place.

To live from the heart with this realized understanding
is to live in the eternal moment
with no past and no future.
Life is now.
This is where a benevolent and empathetic humanity
is not only created but already exists.

Here it becomes clear that cruelty is of a mind
that exists only in time,
as it is the maker of time,
and in this is separated from the wholeness of God,
the eternal consciousness of love.

93 ~ Seek the Eternal

Seek the eternal for the eternal is not something to believe in, rather it is experiential to living from and within the consciousness of love.

94 ~ Existence in the Eternal

There is a natural harmony to our existence.
To be aligned with this harmony is to live from love.
To live from love, harmony occurs naturally.

Harmony in our life stems from the awareness of the source
and living in the consciousness of love.
Allow yourself to stay centered here,
centered in love and alive in harmony with your surroundings.

To develop into your highest potential
you must come to terms with your past and let it go.
You are born anew every day
with nothing binding you to the past.
You are the consciousness of love.
You are unlimited potential for the good of humanity.

The consciousness of love is forever new.
To live from the consciousness of love
is to be continually reborn into every moment anew,
an exchange likened to breathing.
Life is never-endingly received and let go
in one continuous movement.

This is your existence in the eternal now.
Claim this power and live in joy.
It's your destiny.

95 ~ Reborn in Love's Awareness

A person reborn in the consciousness of love's awareness
is a person without a past and sees everything anew.
This is true forgiveness and lies at the center-point of being
in the heart of the consciousness of love.

96 ~ Embrace the Source

Your heart is the fertile ground of the consciousness of love.
This ground is already seeded with benevolence and compassion.
Allow yourself to realize this, as it is the core of your being.
Your mind will follow your heart
when the consciousness of love lights your path.

The unfolding of life is the unfolding of love.
It cannot be controlled, it can only be experienced.
Experience without resistance and you will know freedom.

Embrace the source.
Live in conscious action and be in this world,
as love has embraced and gives conscious rise to you.

97 ~ Magical

When the consciousness of love
is your first and foremost endeavor
your path becomes magical.

98 ~ Deep Inside a Broken Heart

Observe, observe, observe.
You are the eyes of consciousness, the eyes of God.
The action is to observe your mind and nothing more.
This is the change, the ongoing transformation that is you.

The more you observe consciously
the less you act unconsciously.
Let this lift you far beyond the clouds of thought
to a life of clarity, kindness, and compassion.
This is the healing humanity longs for.

Deep inside a broken heart
lies a heart filled with love, laughter, and joy.
One must be broken wide open so the other can be revealed.
Such is the consciousness of love.

99 ~ Allow Your Heart to Weep

Allow your heart to weep as the consciousness of love brings you home.

100 ~ The Grace of Love

You have the power and ability to see through and discern
all the thoughts in your mind.
You are not your mind.
You are that which observes your mind,
and that is the place of contentment and joy.
That is the place that is your heart,
the consciousness of love,
and this is where God dwells.

Allow love to bring your essence
to the never-ending present moment.
Your true essence is gratitude, kindness, and compassion.
Your true self is love.
Be the action of love and humanity will be touched
by your presence.

This is the character and integrity of the divine.
Here, we are unified by the common goodness and grace of love.

101 ~ This Present Moment

What you do in this present moment defines the next.
Allow the consciousness of love to define it for you.

102 ~ Love Is Not Thought

You do not have free will until
you discover love's foundation within you.
It is only from this center-point of awareness,
belonging to love's consciousness,
that you have the ability to discern and choose.
This is the only free will there is.
Otherwise, your will is left to the mind,
and the mind itself has no awareness.

Love is trying to show you all the things you are not.
To be on love's path is a path of negation.
I am not unfulfilled.
I am not depressed.
I am not a victim.
Love is none of these things.

As you return to the center-point of love within you,
you become aware of yourself.
Here, we will see clearly
how we have unconsciously identified ourselves as something,
all because of a thought.
Love is not thought.

Love is a conscious creative energy always expanding within you.
You are a drop in the conscious cosmic ocean of love,
and the entire conscious cosmic ocean is within you.

103 ~ Path of Compassion

To understand your own suffering
is to understand the suffering of humanity.
This is the path of compassion.

104 ~ Ask Yourself

"Struggling to let go" is yet another thought of self-reference.
Ask yourself who you were before the thought arose
that you are identified with.
The you that struggles to let go didn't exist.

You are that which is far beyond thought.
That which observes is without self-reference.
Dare to be without self-reference
and stay in observation as best you can
and "letting go" of anything will vanish.

You are meant to live without suffering
from the torment of your own thought.
Simply observe and nothing more,
and watch a miracle happen within you.

105 ~ Be Still and Observe

Be still and observe, do nothing more.
An endlessly observed mind brings the mind into its alignment with the heart.

106 ~ Healed Humanity

You actually cannot think to yourself who you are.
That is thought using you as its vehicle for expression.
Thought is fleeting and thought passes with the body.
You are not your thoughts.

Thought is meant to be guided by the consciousness of love.
The awareness of thought allows you to "be"...
simply "be"...
without thinking about yourself.
Here, you are fully alive without any need to name yourself.

You are a vehicle for the expression of God,
actuated into beingness by love itself.

Allow the consciousness of love to transform you
from being thought into existence
to being able to consciously discern and choose
a life that benefits all humanity.

We are meant to serve in kindness,
compassion, and benevolence.
This would be a humanity that has healed.

107 ~ The Beauty of Kindness

You possess the ability to live in peace and touch humanity with the love and beauty of kindness.

108 ~ The Eyes of Love's Consciousness

There is nothing to hide and nothing to avoid.
This is the path to self-discovery.
In this lies your remembrance of an unlimited,
fearless being that lives within you
and in direct alignment with the consciousness of love.

The eyes of love's consciousness and your eyes
are one and the same.
See what love sees and act in the ways of love.
Benevolence, compassion, kindness,
and encouragement abounds.

Love's essence is an act of healing that touches all humanity.
It starts within you and reaches
to the depths of the entire cosmos.
Your transcendence affects the whole of creation.

109 ~ Accept the Moment

To be in the moment is to accept the moment
not with thought but within the heart.
Allow your heart to guide your mind.
This is the path to inner peace.

110 ~ Love's Eternal Existence

We have an existence that transcends the physical.
We are an energetic being created by love.
Love is the breath of the entire cosmos,
the breath of existence.

You and I are the breath of loves' existence.
When this is understood
you will look at this world as nothing but love.
You will see yourself and all its creatures
in love's various stages of development.

Live here and love's light will shine its brightest in you.

The consciousness of love does not think about itself,
rather the consciousness of love is aligned with all beings;
therefore, it is an eternal actuation of empathy,
benevolence, and compassion.

Live here and you will be passionately alive
in love's eternal existence.

.

111 ~ Inescapable

If I do ill toward one person,
then I do ill to all humanity.
If I act in kind toward one person,
then I act in kind to all humanity.
This is an inescapable law of love.

112 ~ A Presence of Light

Allow your inner suffering to alter your understanding
of what it is you serve.
To serve your mind is to suffer,
to serve your heart is to live in contentment.
An unobserved mind is the master of a foolish man.
The mind that is observed is a mind that is a servant to the heart
and consciousness of love.

Here, the awakened and conscious life of an individual
flourishes in the eternal presence of now.
There is nothing to control nor is there a need to control.
Every moment of life is filled with deep meaning
as one is fully present to this unfolding of life.
The simple beauty of kindness in speech and action
is naturally first and foremost in an awakened being.

Love is the foundation and home of the heart.
An individual that has awakened
and has allowed their mind to align with their heart
lives in an inner kingdom of peace, contentment, and love.
Such an individual is a presence of light to all he meets.

113 ~ Riches of the Heart

Love in such a way that you need not have that love reciprocated.
Love this way and you will receive riches of the heart
that cannot be imagined.

114 ~ Love's Apprentice

As I speak and as I act, so I create.
My words and actions are the essence
of my journey to this exact moment,
my steps into the next.

If I cannot speak in kindness and act with compassion,
then where would kindness and compassion
reciprocate itself to me?
My world is the reflection of the level of my understanding.

I have learned there is only one language and one action...
Love.

I am love's apprentice.
My prayer is compassion.
My actions are of kindness.
My words are of peace.

I am but a breath of love's existence,
and because of this I know no other way to live.

115 ~ An Infinite Well

Let the wounds of this world speak to your heart
and show you how much love you can give.
Love is an infinite well of divine consciousness.
The more you use it the more you receive.

116 ~ The Foundation of Peace

A person that serves their thoughts and thoughts only
is easily deceived by another person
that serves their thoughts and thoughts only.
This is the blind leading the blind.

To break free one must see through
the deception of their own mind.
In doing so one returns
to the awareness of the consciousness of love.
This is the alignment with the divine
that is our natural state of being.
This is our true home.

If you could see you are not your thoughts
you would then know love.
Love gives rise to the awareness
that is the vision and action of freedom.
True freedom lies within the human being
who has transcended his thoughts
and acts from the never-ending awareness of love.

Herein lies the freedom from negative thinking,
the foundation of peace.

117 ~ The Peace You Are Searching For

The peace you are searching for does not exist outside of you.

118 ~ Love Will Draw You Out

Though it may be perceived by the mind as sad or happy,
painful or joyful, good or bad,
love does not define any experience.
Love observes and lets the experience be.

This is love in conscious action: egoless,
the ground of mindfulness,
and freedom from an imagined reality
of what should or shouldn't be.

The consciousness of love will draw you out of this world.
You will be in this world but not of it's making
nor under its authority.

Love will be your constitution,
and the essence of love will emanate
from the light of love within you.

119 ~ Power and Grace

You have the power to love
without being owed anything in return.
Such power and grace dwell within all of us.
Let nothing hold you back!

120 ~ Love is the Courage

War does not keep peace.
No amount of cruelty ever left an impression of peace,
only sorrow.
And war returns.

We have long forgotten that we belong to each other.
Peace is first realized within the human being
that lives from the foundation of love.
The weapons for all conflict are empathy, kindness,
compassion, and forgiveness.

To walk the path of the peaceful warrior
is to bring light into the darkness
so that what is unknowingly hidden
can experience the illumination, receive the love,
and seize the opportunity to transcend the darkness
in which they dwell.

Love is the courage and lives within the heart
of the individual who has awakened.

121 ~ The Heart That Lives in Love

It is not the mind that understands love
but the heart that lives in love.

122 ~ Love's Pure Perception

Love invites us out of a life of the imagined structures
we have come to take as real
and into the pure perception of reality as it is.

Here, we see and experience life from a deeper and higher view,
centered within our hearts
and aware of our thoughts that are anchored
by these imagined structures.

In reality, we are unlimited potential,
unhindered by any negative states
we have unknowingly conceptualized.

Love is not lacking in anything.
It is whole by its very nature.
It is not an entity of hate, greed, or injustice.

The essence of love is wholeness, unity, and oneness.
Kindness, compassion, encouragement, forgiveness, and grace
all flow from love.

Humanity's thirst for peace can only be quenched by love.
Return home to the consciousness of love,
the healing of humanity lies within you.

123 ~ Love Must Be My Action

Recognize your life as love.
Recognize all life as love.
How could you harm it?
I can see with all my heart love is what I am.
Therefore, love must be my action.

124 ~ Infinite Possibilities

There is no greater catastrophe
than a human being who has let the world tell him who he is.
Dive into the depths of yourself,
and there you will find a sunken treasure.

Allow yourself to be replaced with the consciousness of love.
Things that once seemed to be impossible
become not only possible
but a path to take will appear before you.

It's okay to let go.
You are letting go of your mind's hold on you
and trusting your heart.

To trust your heart is to trust the consciousness of love
that dwells within you.
Don't be concerned over what will replace what you let go of.

Infinite abundance and endless possibilities thrive
when held in the heart of the one who has let go
and serves love.

125 ~ When the Magic Happens

When there is no more resistance to "what is"
that's when the magic happens and you become the magician
for the good of not only your life
but the good of all humanity.

126 ~ The Key That Unlocks the Door

There IS such a thing as a loving,
conscious intelligence.
It is alive and has been eternally waiting in silence
within you for your discovery.
Whether you discover it or not,
it is there and will always be there.

The awareness of the consciousness of love is who you are.
It is its own fulfillment,
whole and complete.

When you realize with all your heart
that you are standing endlessly before God,
the consciousness of love,
abandonment of self is instantaneous and effortless.

This is the key that unlocks the door of discovery
to unlimited beingness for the good of all things.

127 ~ Seek the Eternal

Seek the eternal for the eternal is not something to believe in, rather it is experiential to living from and within the consciousness of love.

128 ~ The Awakened Human Being

Your soul has nothing to do with your ego
but has everything to do in conjunction with
your awakened heart and the consciousness of love.

The authenticity of love's consciousness is egoless.
You aren't at all who you think you are,
for there is no self-reference when living from love,
the divine center of being.

This center-point of being permeates the cosmos.
The awakened human being is in this world
and simultaneously aware of and in all worlds
throughout the cosmic whole.
One is aware of their words, actions, and thoughts
as they ripple throughout the space-time continuum.

The awakened human being
is incited by the consciousness of love
for the good of all life.

Ultimately words do not do justice
when talking about the consciousness of love.
For the true seeker of the divine,
the one who would awaken,
truth will unfold.

129 ~ The Path to Awakening

The path to awakening is not a path in time,
it is never-endingly now.

130 ~ My Journey in This Life

Make your foundation that of love
and become conscious of love's requests upon you.
Kindness, compassion, and empathy
will light not only your own path
but also the paths of many.

As long as I live from the consciousness of love,
the center-point of being,
my journey in this life will be filled with joy and contentment.
It matters not what I want,
rather what I give.

Treat everyone as if they were you.
They are.
The consciousness of humanity is affected by each individual.
We are of one consciousness.

131 ~ Love Isn't Hiding

Love isn't hiding.
Simply close your eyes and see with your heart.
The source of this beautiful mystery lies within you.

132 ~ A Mind That Is Free

Thought's purpose is to serve the heart.
Without the awareness and guidance of the heart,
thought is limited and constricting.
A mind that is free is a mind that is observed.

One must go through their own inner darkness
to reach the light within them.
The consciousness of love dwells within every individual
and it is here where humanity will heal.

Know yourself and you will know humanity.
Allow yourself to transcend your mind
and you will have the most active and loving part
in helping humanity heal and know peace.

133 ~ Peace and Healing

Allow your heart to quiet your mind
and know the peace and healing of the consciousness of love.

134 ~ The Extraordinary

There is a kingdom of peace that resides
at the center-point of being.
Here, a lighthouse of pure observation fulfills its role
in providing you the vision to see all that you are
and all that you are not not.

Your thoughts cannot create happiness.
Only serving your heart
and allowing the awareness of thought to pass
can happiness ever be realized.

Happiness is the actuation of love's consciousness
realized within an individual who is ready
for something more than just ordinary,
familiar human thought.

The consciousness of love is celestial and divine.
When you have no more need to serve the ordinary
the extraordinary will be waiting.

135 ~ Beneath the Wreckage

Beneath the wreckage of a collapsed structure
of who I thought I was
arose the consciousness of love.

136 ~ The Abyss of Freedom

You cannot serve your mind and your heart at the same time.
To serve your mind is to sacrifice your heart.
To serve your heart is to enlighten your mind.

Why toil with your thoughts about life
when you can embrace love's heart and abandon yourself.
Acquiesce and fall into the divine arms of love.

Let it occur to you that you need not listen to yourself thinking.
The ground of observation is pure silence.
Let silence take you to the edge of the world of thought...
then jump into the abyss of freedom.

137 ~ You Hold the World

You hold the world in your heart,
let not your mind get in the way.

138 ~ Your Soul's Desire

The fulfillment you seek is not outside of you.
The action of thought is that it needs to search,
but you are not thought.

The moment you start to seek you leave your heart.
The consciousness of love needs nothing to be fulfilled,
as it is its own fulfillment.

Be still.
Allow the silence of simply "being" to envelop you.
There is thunder in this silence,
the thunder of God breathing you into existence.

The gift of this existence comes with responsibility.
Allow your heart to awaken as it is your soul's desire
and your soul's desire is why you are here.

139 ~ Celestial and Eternal

There is no beginning to the consciousness of love
and there is no end.
You are the seed of this consciousness,
celestial and eternal.

140 ~ Guided by the Heart

Inner silence leads to peace,
both inwardly and outwardly.
They are identical.
A quiet mind is realized within a human being
residing within the consciousness of love's awareness.

When consciousness guides the mind to stillness,
love is revealed,
and the illusion of the identification
with thought is understood.
Here, thought is guided by the heart
in alignment with the divine.

Silence is at the center-point of observation.
Remain in inner silence and observe.
Here, life is now allowed to unfold naturally as it's meant to.
Thought is not struggled with, no narration needed.
Simply discerned and dismissed.
Guidance is of the consciousness of love.

141 ~ The Greatest Prayer

The greatest prayer is silence
for it fulfills the heart
and heals the mind.

142 ~ The Healing of Humanity

There is no denying this human race is suffering.
We are out of balance with our true nature.
We, as a human race, cannot come to balance as a whole
without first coming to balance as individuals within the whole.

Therefore, I must be an action of balance.
I must be an action of love.
At all costs, I should rather cease living
than to hurt another in action or in thought.

A sane mind is a mind guided by
the awareness of the consciousness of love.
A sane mind has no ill will,
none.

This is the action of the consciousness of love.
This is the healing of humanity of which we are all responsible.

143 ~ Love This World

You can help someone or hurt someone.
It's that simple.
And if you can't help someone,
you have it within you to not hurt them.
Therefore, you have more power to love this world
than to hurt it.

144 ~ Peace Exists

Peace exists.
We have strayed from the peace we already are.
Peace exists prior to thinking.
The consciousness of love observes and discerns.
Here there is no hate, no war, no greed, and no deception.

The consciousness of love which dwells in all human beings
resolves all inner and outer conflict.
You were born with the spiritual eyes to see and ears to hear,
which is the foundation of love's conscious awareness
of yourself.

Hand your story over to God
and be with nothing to define yourself.
This is the ground of a new life,
one of which cannot be imagined.
This is the ground on which you are meant
to walk your path set before you.

Live from the awareness of the consciousness of love.
The human being that lives here is a light of peace.

145 ~ Guided by Love

I am guided by love.
If it is unkind, I will not speak it.
If it is hateful, I will not act.
The laws of love are simple.
They are written in our hearts.
If I am not living from my heart, I am not living from love.

146 ~ Love Is My Path

I have remembered what I am.
I am the eyes that see inwardly all that is true and untrue.
Discernment is easy and all is let go.

I have but one need, the divine nature of love.
All other needs pass in a temporary world of existence.

You can find me in the field where love perceives life.
Outside of this field perception is tainted
with our mind's imagination.

I am driven to be fully alive and awake
the moment this body passes; hence,
I have surrendered to the consciousness of love.

I am resolved to speak words that uplift humanity
else I shall not speak.
My actions shall be that of kindness and encouragement
else I shall not act.

Love is my path.
Love is my soul's ardent endeavor.
All else pales in comparison.

147 ~ You Are Humanity

Raise the level of your actions and raise the level of humanity. You ARE humanity.

148 ~ We Are Creation and Creators

Come to the understanding that currently
your identity of who you are
is a mask worn over consciousness.
You are not the mask, you are consciousness.

Through your own observation of your mind,
it will be revealed to you the unlimited potential
of who and what you really are.

At the center-point of beingness lies the awareness
of the unlimited potential that resides in all human beings.
The consciousness of love is unendingly expanding its creation
through which humanity and the cosmic whole exist.

We ARE creation,
and we ARE creators.

149 ~ Paint the Canvas of Your Soul

Paint the canvas of your soul with the consciousness of love.
The colors of the consciousness of love
are to awaken what lies dormant within you,
a heart filled with kindness, compassion, contentment, and joy.

150 ~ Moved by Love's Grace

The eyes to see inwardly is all that is required
for the journey home to your true self.

Allow the sky of your mind
to be lit by the consciousness of love
no longer thinking for itself,
rather in alignment with and guided by the heart.

The peace and healing of humanity
resides in every person on the planet.

We have the ability to wake up as individuals
and treat our fellow man with benevolence,
kindness, compassion, empathy, and encouragement
and the beauty is we need nothing owed to us in return.

The awakened individual is moved by love's grace
and lives within the consciousness of a sacred life
that reaches into the cosmos.

151 ~ Love's Servant

You are love's servant.
Did you forget?
Just surrender.
Surrender to serving love,
and you will return to a life of joy beyond measure.

152 ~ Path to Peace

The path you walk is actuated through your awareness
of the consciousness of love.
By this, as you speak and act,
your path is a never-ending creation
of your connectedness to the divine.
Allow the living action of love's benevolence
to create your path and touch humanity.

The whole of space is alive and intrinsically connected.
Its energy is the foundation of your beating heart.
It is your heart that is your guiding light.
Allow your mind to be silent and follow.

Where you are at this very moment,
love has been waiting for you.
Love has graced this moment with its essence
and has extended an open invitation for you
to enter into a new life.

Herein lies the path to peace.

153 ~ A Life of Love

A life of love is not to be found but realized.
I already am the love I want to find.

154 ~ The Well Is Within You

You are being called to the source of happiness.
It has nothing to do with what you want
but everything to do with what you need.
If you follow this call,
you will discover what you need IS what you want.

What do you need?
To live from the source of the will of love.

The entire cosmos is alive and empowering you
to be actuated by the consciousness of love
for it IS the consciousness of love.

In the midst of the chaotic mind there is a silence,
like a hidden, natural well within you awaiting its discovery.
Drink from the well of the consciousness of love.
Your soul thirsts and the well is within you.

This is your destiny.

155 ~ Given Everything

When realized, you are given everything
because you are everything.

156 ~ Born Without Limits

The limits you believe you now have
are an acquired conditioned perception
based on the unconscious use of your imagination.
Over time it's become a familiar and unchallenged concept.
This belief has become your reality.
It's not true.

You cannot think yourself out of the suffering
you have thought yourself into,
but you can observe yourself out of the whole equation.

The path to freedom is discovering
there is nothing worth holding onto.
Nothing binds you to yesterday,
for you are born every day anew.

You were born without limits.
It's just that simple.

157 ~ That Which Is Before Thought

You are that which is before thought,
the ground of awareness.
Reside in that which is before thought and suffering will cease.

158 ~ Effortlessly Present

There is no need to be burdened by thought.
Thought is to be understood and discerned
through the eyes of awareness of the consciousness of love.

It's impossible for thought to define who you are
and what you should feel.
You have the power as the consciousness of love itself
to observe.
Here, you serve the heart.

To truly live in the now is to live in an awareness
of inner stillness and observation.
This awareness is in direct alignment
with the consciousness of love.
All identification with judgments and opinions
are seen as worthless and wasted energy.
The awakened individual wastes no time
in such meaningless thoughts and actions.

Endeavor to be effortlessly present to yourself,
as the consciousness of love will endlessly incite
your speech and actions.

Live from the consciousness of love,
the healing of humanity lies within you.

159 ~ The Eternal Now

Your life is not meant to be lived
chained to the memory of the past
but in the freedom of the eternal now.

160 ~ Breathed Into Existence

My home is not of this earth.
This I am positive.
We are all a celestial seed, and we will return to the celestial.
Our path is celestial.
Love designed this path, for the celestial IS love.

Be true to this path for it is your sacred journey.
Return to the consciousness of love,
for that you where it started.

You are not a product of thought.
You are a creation of the divine and celestial
consciousness of love.

You are being breathed into existence,
and you are breathing in the consciousness of love.
Your breath and the air you breath is one entity, love.

Love is the energetic, ethereal composition of space itself.
There is no existence without love.
It is the heartbeat of life and the expansion of the cosmos.

Return to the celestial consciousness of love.
Live benevolently and charitably.
Know the sweet joy of living in peace.

161 ~ The Sky of Your Heart

Dance in the sky of your heart self-realized in love.

162 ~ Anything Is Possible With Love

I stood alone in the desert and looked toward the sky.
My broken heart was mended.
Weakness was given strength.
Cowardice was given courage.
Arrogance replaced with humility.
Hate was shown forgiveness.
My eyes had a new view.
A view so high that what I took myself to be
was utterly insignificant.
There is only love.
And life in union with love replaced me,
and I was shown anything is possible with love.

I don't live in this world.
I live in love's world.
The world of love has graced me with the heart
to live in and love this world.
Hence, I am in this world,
but I am not of this world.

In the midst of the chaotic mind of this human race
I see the possibilities,
I live the possibilities,
and my path is eternally lit
by the consciousness of love for all mankind.

163 ~ One Path

I have but one responsibility, love.
I have but one prayer, love.
I have but one gift, love.
I have but one path, love.

164 ~ Just For Today

Negativity is an unconscious state of being.
How is this so?
A human being in negativity is identified with and serving
a mind left to its own wanderings.

This is a mind unanchored
by the awareness of the consciousness of love.
Our true home is the center-point of observation
within the consciousness of love.

From here, the mind is observed without identification.
Here, one can discern all thoughts passing through the mind.
This is the guidance of the consciousness of love.
This is the awareness from which we heal ourselves
and humanity.

Dare to be without any negativity about anything whatsoever.
Let the light shine that dwells within your heart.
The whole world will be affected by this one conscious act
and its effect will ripple throughout the cosmos.

165 ~ Love Will Be Waiting

When you tire of following your negative thought patterns
into the abyss of your all-too-familiar suffering
love will be waiting for you.

166 ~ My Prayer Is Simple

I never tire of searching.
Where will you show up next?
And then I remember you are right here.
You always have been,
closer to me than my own breath.

Yet, I will forget.
You know I will forget,
and you never stop loving me.
You breathe me into existence.
This life is yours that lives not mine.

My prayer is simple: Love, please replace me with you.

167 ~ Love Is My Religion

It's quite simple; love is my religion.

168 ~ Dancing With God

There is no past or future outside of this moment,
for the very moment is eternal.
Whatever I put my attention on
I will either experience suffering or joy,
as all there is to experience is all at this moment.

If my attention stems from the consciousness of love,
then my awareness directs my attention
and discernment of thought.
Here, as all thought is observed,
I am now able to release thought,
see beyond thought,
and peace and joy are fully experienced.
When this is experientially realized mental anguish ceases.

When you are living fully and unendingly present
in this beautiful, eternal moment
you then live guided by your heart
and your life becomes a dance.

You are dancing with God.

169 ~ Be Your Own Teacher

Be your own teacher and walk your own path.
Walk with an open heart in peace, gratitude,
kindness, and forgiveness.

About the Author

David is a first-time author and long time practitioner of living in the now, a conscious seeker of truth for the past 35 years. He feels we all desire the same thing, to live in the consciousness of love. One of David's deepest passions of his heart is to share with others, on a similar or different journey, all the magic life has to offer.

David's life was anything but magical at the age of 55. After having been in the ICU for ten days, he woke up to a life of joblessness, homelessness, and worst of all unrelenting shame and a desire to not be here anymore. He lived out of his car for close to three months, showered at the local YMCA, and lived on a daily diet of fast-food and uncertainty. This was at an age in life where the majority of people were planning for retirement. He had lost all belief that he'd recover or, sorrowfully, ever want to.

In the face of having completely given up at that precise moment, one of the most beautiful gifts was about to be given to him, the gift of surrender. Standing on a hill, David threw his arms up in the air and cried out, "Father, I have failed. I cannot take my own life. I do not want to wake up tomorrow, so you can take it for me tonight." The next morning he awoke to a feeling that was unlike any other he had felt before. Something was different and yet distinctively unfamiliar and nameless. The epiphany, as he calls it, was that he indisputably knew that he was responsible for every decision, every pain, everything that had taken place in his life. This external illusion was his creation. The truth he so fervently sought for over 30 years was now alive within, and he knew his path to this moment was perfect.

With this new understanding, David was able to choose consciously and be attached to nothing. Life was nothing but unlimited potential. He now understood that with God anything was possible. This is when life's magic began to unfold, and unfold did it ever. David was blessed with an incredible career at one of the nation's leading online continuing education companies. As an acoustic and electric guitarist and composer, he has released 11 solo albums. And now the release of his first book "Signs Along The Path To Awakening." At the age of 60, David feels his life is just beginning.

Others undeniably sense the joy which flows from his heart as a result of simply being present in the now. David is a walking, breathing example that anything is possible when you accept responsibility for your thoughts, which ultimately determines your outcome. He hopes to touch people's hearts across the globe through his writings. He is consciously dedicated to sharing the love which resides in each and every one of us.

Contact:

DavidModicaWritings.com - Here you will find the latest writings, videos, and inspiration to help you along your journey.

On Facebook - David Modica: Writings on Spirituality

David invites you to email him at: djmwritings@gmail.com

Lightning Source UK Ltd.
Milton Keynes UK
UKHW010650210820
368569UK00002B/112/J